puppyknits

12 QuickKnit Fashions for Your Best Friend

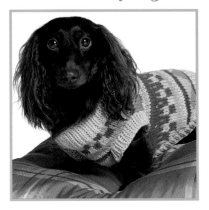

Jil Eaton

Breckling Press

Library of Congress Cataloging-in-Publication Data
Eaton, Jil, 1949–
   PuppyKnits : 12 QuickKnit fashions for your best friend / Jil Eaton.
      p. cm.
   "A Minnowknits book."
   ISBN 1-933308-06-0
   1. Knitting—Patterns. 2 Dogs—Equipment and supplies. 3. Sweaters.
I. Title.

   TT825.E286 2005
      746.43'20432—dc22

                                                          2005016860

This book was set in Scala Sans by Bartko Design, Inc.
Printed in China

Every effort has been made to be accurate and complete with all the information in this book. The publisher and the author cannot be responsible for differences in knitters' abilities, typographical errors, techniques, tools or conditions or any resulting damages or mistakes or losses.

Editorial direction by Anne Knudsen
Cover and interior design by Kim Bartko
Photography direction by Jil Eaton
Cover and interior photographs by Nina Fuller
Styling by Isabel Smiles, Annie Brown, Tunde Schwartz, and Jil Eaton
Pattern design by Jil Eaton
Learn-to-knit illustrations by Joni Coniglio
Drawings by Jil Eaton
Schematics by Jane Fay
Technical writing and editing by Carla Scott
Pattern proofing by Janice Bye
Knit samples by Nita Young, Shirley LaBranch, Lucinda Heller, Carol Lawrence, Pam Tessier, and Jil Eaton

Published by Breckling Press, a division of Knudsen, Inc.
283 Michigan Street, Elmhurst, IL 60126, USA

Dedication

To Zachary, my beloved thirteen-year-old pooch, an enormous
one-hundred-and-six-pound Dane/Greyhound/Pointer who we
rescued from a shelter. Zach keeps me company in the studio, takes
me for walks in every imaginable kind of weather, forgives all my
transgressions, and is my very own "girl's best friend."

Contents

Woof!

Fido . . . Lassie . . . man's best friend . . . girl's best friend, for that matter. Is there any limit to our pooch love? Is there anything we wouldn't do for our fabulous furry companions? *PuppyKnits* is exactly what today's best-dressed doggies are looking for. Colorful and luxurious, these ultra-chic knits can be whipped up in a flash. When it's cold outside your best friend needs toasty toppers, perfect for peeking out of the carry-all as you gad around town together. Perky and chic, easily knit but with delightful details, these adorable tidbits are enchanting fashion statements for your beloved pets. Remember, when we are knitting, all is right with the world.

Jil Eaton

Jil Eaton
Portland, Maine

The Dog-Gone Idea

The inspiration for *PuppyKnits* came from the streets of
New York and Chicago, where dogs are loved and petted
and primped, carried and shopped, and always adorned in
the best finery. I've published individual patterns for dogs
before and they are always popular. Why not, I thought,
create an entire collection for the canine set, chic, charming,
and complete with buttons and bows, ruffles and fringe? I
quickly discovered that we can never knit too much for our
petites chiens!

I always use the highest quality yarns available in a rich
range of colors, and this collection of doggie knits is no
exception. Natural fibers make the best sweaters, as the fibers
breathe and felt and wear like iron. The yardage is given both
in English and metric, with information on the actual yarns
used, to allow you flexibility as you make your own knitting
design decisions. Your miniature Pekinese, for instance,
may look better in a totally different colorway than on our
Daschund. Beautiful yarns make a beautiful project, inside
and out, and can never be too good for our precious pooches.

If you are a beginner or even a veteran knitter, here
are some of my tried and true ideas for happy knitting
adventures. Sometimes the smallest changes in your
repertoire will bring harmony to your knitting life, and you'll
have more time to walk the dog.

Knitting to Fit

Pooches come in all shapes and sizes. While all the designs in *PuppyKnits* are intended for small dogs, each breed has its own peculiarities. To make sure your finished garment fits comfortably, pay close attention to the following preparatory steps.

GETTING THE GAUGE

The single most important step when beginning any knitting project is to do a gauge swatch. The gauge swatch is a 4"/ (10 cm) square, knit in the pattern called for and with the

Knitting Kit

A clear zippered case, like those used for cosmetics, is best for the perfect knitting kit. Everything is visible and it's easy to fish out items you need. If you set yourself up with the following items, you have a portable studio, easily stashed in your knitting bag as you change venues or projects.

* Small, very sharp scissors, used only for yarn.
* Yarn needles: I like the Japanese Chibi needles with bent tips.
* Retractable measuring tape.
* Yarn T-pins and yarn safety pins for marking or holding dropped stitches.
* Stitch holders, both long and short. English Aeros are my favorites, but Japanese holders that are open at either end are also fabulous.

recommended needle size. Getting the correct gauge, or number of stitches per inch, allows you to make a fabric that is even and smooth, with the correct drape and hand, resulting in the correct size. Any garment that is off-gauge by just one stitch per inch may end up five inches too big or too small for your pup! Experienced knitters may tell you they always knit to gauge—don't believe it. Everyone knits differently with different yarns, needles and patterns. The bottom line is that if you want happy results every time, do your gauge swatch!

Using the needles suggested in the pattern, cast on the correct number of stitches to make a 4"/10 cm swatch, plus six more stitches. Knit three rows. Always knit three stitches

* Stitch markers: split-rings are good as they can be easily moved and removed.
* Cable needles: I use straight US sizes 3, 6 and 10.
* Point protectors, both large and small, to keep your work on the needles.
* Needle/gauge ruler—essential.
* Crochet hooks: one small, one large
* "Dentists tool," with one hooked end and one smooth end—invaluable.
* Pen and small notebook, for notes, figuring and design notes.
* Small calculator, which you will use constantly.

Sammy 2006

13" COLLAR

10" UNDER COLLAR TO END OF RIBS

13"–16" CENTER BACK

18½" CHEST

at the beginning and end of every row, and work straight in the pattern stitches called for until the piece measures 4"/10 cm. Knit three more rows and bind off. Lay the swatch on a flat, smooth surface. Measure inside the garter stitch frame; you should have 4"/10 cm exactly. If your swatch is too big, or you have too few stitches per inch, change to a needle one size smaller. If your swatch is too small, or there are too many stitches per inch, change to the next larger needles. Getting into the habit of doing your gauge swatch will fine-tune your craftsmanship, making you a better knitter for life.

MEASURING YOUR PUP

Dogs come in myriad shapes and sizes—round or long or skinny or chubby, furry or bald. or curly and fluffy. No two are alike, so inventing sizing templates has been as challenging as measuring the squirmy little critters! The sweaters in *PuppyKnits* were designed to fit the particular dogs photographed, and we have sized them according to the various breeds. So you really must carefully measure your own pooch to make sure there's a comfortable fit.

There are the two basic shapes used for this collection of dog sweaters and jackets. Look over the schematics below to determine where you need to measure your dog in order to make any adjustments to the pattern.

Shape One

Shape One is a pullover sweater worked from the neck to the tail, with a seam down the center of the under belly. The leg openings are bound-off then each section is worked separately for a few inches. You then cast on new stitches above the bind-offs and work even to the tail shaping. Be sure to measure your dog carefully, including the width between the legs. If your dog has a lot of fur or has chubby legs, you may want a bigger opening. If your dog has very little fur, you may want to use fewer stitches in the bind-off.

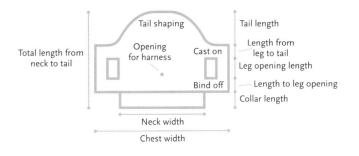

Shape Two

Shape Two is a jacket that buttons around the neck, with underbelly straps. It is worked and shaped from the tail to the neck. After the garment is finished, try it on your pup to determine where you should pick up stitches to knit the straps. We have included measurements for the strap placement, but it is easy to move them so your dog is more comfy.

We noticed that most of these little charmers sport a harness, so we have included an option for working buttonholes to accommodate the leash hook. You might

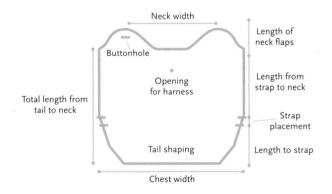

Neck width

Length of
neck flaps

Buttonhole

Opening
for harness

Length from
strap to neck

Total length from
tail to neck

Strap
placement

Tail shaping

Length to strap

Chest width

want to measure your own puppy's gear and adjust that opening accordingly.

BLOCKING FINISHED PIECES

When you complete a project, cover each piece with two damp towels, one under and one over, pinning the pieces in place. Alternatively, you may pin the pieces to a blocking board, a wonderful invention that is widely available. Lightly steam at the appropriate setting for the yarn you are using, and dry your garment flat on a towel, mesh rack, or on the blocking board. Blocking usually improves the look of your garment, as long as it is gently done.

CARING FOR DOGGIE KNITS

You will want to launder your doggie sweaters, and your gauge swatches are absolutely perfect for testing the washability of a specific yarn, following the yarn label instructions. Most yarns are machine washable, if you put them on a very gentle cycle in tepid water. Place them in a small mesh bag, which allows the garments to hold their shape while getting them really clean. For wool, you should also use a no-rinse sweater soap such as Eucalan, which is available at fine yarn shops as well as on the Internet.

Learn to Knit

This learn-to-knit section takes you through the basic elements of knitting. Although there are many others, I have included only two types of cast-ons, the *knit-on cast-on* and the *cable cast-on*. Once you have mastered the knit-on method, you have actually learned the basic knit stitch. The cable cast-on is a variation on the same stitch and is used to form a sturdy, yet elastic edge.

SLIP KNOT

1. Hold the yarn in your left hand, leaving a short length free. Wrap the yarn from the skein into a circle and bring the yarn from below and up through the center of the circle. Insert the needle under this strand as shown.

2. Pull on both the short and long ends to tighten the knot on the needle.

STEP 1. *Slip Knot*

STEP 2. *Slip Knot*

STEP 1. *Cast-On*

STEP 2. *Cast-On*

STEP 3. *Cast-On*

KNIT-ON CAST-ON

1. Hold the needle with the slipknot in the left hand and the empty needle in the right hand. Insert the right needle from front to back under the left needle and through the stitch. With the yarn in the right hand, wrap the yarn around the right needle as shown.

2. With the tip of the right needle, pull the wrap through the stitch on the left needle and bring to the front.

3. Slip the new stitch off of the right needle and onto the left needle. Repeat steps 1 to 3 for a simple knit-on cast-on.

STEP 1. *Cable Cast-On*

CABLE CAST-ON

1. Insert the right needle between the first two stitches on the left needle and wrap the yarn around the needle as shown.

2. With the tip of the right needle, pull the wrap through to the front.

3. Slip the new stitch off the left needle and onto the right needle. Repeat steps 1 to 3 for a cable cast-on.

STEP 1. *Basic Knit Stitch*   **STEP 2.** *Basic Knit Stitch*

BASIC KNIT STITCH

1. Hold the needle with the cast-on stitches in the left hand and hold the empty needle in the right hand. Insert the right needle from front to back into the first stitch on the left needle and wrap the yarn just like in the first step of the cast-on.

2. With the tip of the right needle, pull the wrap through the stitch on the left needle and onto the right needle. Drop the stitch from the left needle. A new stitch is made on the right needle. Repeat steps 1 and 2 until all the stitches from the left needle are on the right needle. Turn the work and hold the needle with the new stitches in the left hand and continue knitting back and forth.

BASIC PURL STITCH

The purl stitch is the opposite of the knit stitch. Instead of pulling the wrapped yarn towards you, you will push it through the back of the stitch. Because it is harder to see what you are doing, the purl stitch is a bit harder to learn than the knit stitch.

STEP 1. *Basic Purl Stitch*

1. Hold the needle with the cast-on stitches in the left hand and the empty needle in the right hand. Insert the right needle from back to front, into the first stitch on the left needle, and wrap the yarn counter-clockwise around the needle as shown.

2. With the tip of the right needle, pull the wrap through the stitch on the left needle and onto the right needle, as in the knit stitch. Drop the stitch from the left needle. A new stitch is made on the right needle. Continue in this way across the row.

STOCKINETTE STITCH

On straight needles, knit on the right side, purl on the wrong side. On a circular needle, knit every round.

GARTER STITCH

When knitting with straight needles, knit every row. On a circular needle, knit one round, purl one round.

DECREASE OR KNIT TWO TOGETHER (K2TOG)

Knit Two Together

Hold the needle with the knitted fabric in the left hand and hold the empty needle in the right hand. Insert the right needle from front to back through the first two stitches on the left needle. Wrap the yarn and pull through the two stitches as if knitting. Drop the two stitches from the left needle. One new stitch is made from two stitches; therefore one stitch is decreased.

INCREASE

Knit in the front of the stitch, and, without removing the stitch from the left hand needle, knit in the back of the same stitch, then drop the stitches from the left needle. This makes two stitches in one stitch.

BIND OFF

Hold the needle with the knitting in the left hand and hold the empty needle in the right hand. Knit the first two stitches. *With the left needle in front of the right needle, insert the tip of the left needle into the second stitch on the right needle and pull it over the first stitch and off the right needle. One stitch has been bound off. Knit the next stitch, then repeat from the * until all the stitches are bound off.

Bind Off

Cabled Delight

*Here's a classic look, perfect for the Ivy League set. Cable is one
of my favorite techniques. The three-dimensional quality makes a
garment that lofts, trapping air for extra warmth. With the cable
row coming back every eight rows, this is a pattern that holds
your interest to the very last stitch.*

●●● **INTERMEDIATE QUICKKNIT**

Finished chest: 11½ (14 – 16¼ – 18¾)"/29 (35.5 – 41 – 47.5) cm
Length, neck to tail: 9 (10 – 12 – 14)"/23 (25.5 – 30.5 – 35.5) cm

MATERIALS

Worsted weight yarn: 90 (120 – 170 – 225) yards/80 (110 –
155 – 205) meters
Straight needles: sizes 6 and 8 US (8 and 6 UK; 4 mm and
5 mm)
Double-pointed needle (dpns), set of four: size 6 (8 UK; 4 mm)
Cable needle (cn)
Stitch holder and markers

GAUGE

26 sts and 26 rows = 4"/10 cm over cable pattern using
larger needles

✔ *Always check gauge to save time and ensure correct yardage.
Adjust needle size as necessary (see page 4).*

Puppy Profile

NAME: Griffin, age 2
BREED: Yorkshire Terrier
INTERESTS: Chewing, soccer,
watching *Bonanza* re-runs
STYLE: "A cozy fit that slides
easily over my paws and ears—
styling's important, but warmth
matters, too."
*Griffin, assistant inn-keeper at his
parent's family B&B, sports a one-
piece cabled sweater knit in Manos
del Uruguay, #66, red. This is
a wonderful roving yarn, hand
made and dyed on a collective in
Uruguay. The colors are fabulous,
and the yarn has a soft hand.*

Cable Pattern

(MULTIPLE OF 8 STS PLUS 2)

Row 1 (RS): p2, *k6, p2; repeat
   from * to end

Rows 2, 4, 6, and 8: k all knit
   stitches and p all purl
   stitches

Row 3: p2, *sl 3 sts to cn and
   hold to back of work, k3, k3
   from cn, p2; repeat from *
   to end

Rows 5 and 7: repeat row 1

Repeat rows 1 to 8 for cable
   pattern

BODY

1. With smaller needles, cast on 54 (60 – 72 – 84) sts
for neck and work in k1, p1 rib for 1.5"/4 cm. Increase 20
(30 – 34 – 38) sts evenly across last (WS) row to 74 (90 –
106 – 122) sts.

2. Change to larger needles. Work in cable pattern until
piece measures 2½ (3 – 3 – 3½)"/6.5 (7.5 – 7.5 – 9) cm from
beginning, ending with a WS row. See option.

SPLIT FOR LEG OPENING

3. *Next row (RS)*: work 8 (8 – 9 – 9) sts, then place
remaining sts on a holder. Continue on these 8 (8 – 9 – 9)
sts only for 2 (2 – 2½ – 3)"/5 (5 – 6.5 – 7.5) cm, ending with a
RS row. Place sts on a second holder. Cut yarn.

4. Rejoin yarn and bind off next 7 (9 – 9 – 9) sts from first
holder for leg opening, then work next 44 (56 – 70 – 86) sts
only for 2 (2 – 2½ – 3)"/5 (5 – 6.5 – 7.5) cm, ending with a RS
row. Place sts on a third holder. Cut yarn.

5. Rejoin yarn and bind off next 7 (9 – 9 – 9) sts from first
holder for leg opening. Work remaining 8 (8 – 9 – 9) sts for
2 (2 – 2½ – 3)"/5 (5 – 6.5 – 7.5) cm, ending with a RS row.

6. *Next row (WS)*: work 8 (8 – 9 – 9) sts from needle. Cast
on 7 (9 – 9 – 9) sts, then work 44 (56 – 70 – 86) sts from
third holder. Cast on 7 (9 – 9 – 9) sts , then work remaining
8 (8 – 9 – 9) sts from second holder. Continue on all stitches
until piece measures 6 (6½ – 8 – 9½)"/15.5 (16.5 – 20.5 –
24) cm or desired length from beginning.

TAIL SHAPING

7. Bind off 8 (10 – 10 – 11) sts at beginning of next two rows. Decrease 1 st each side *every* row, 12 (14 – 18 – 22) times. Bind off 4 (4 – 4 – 5) sts at beginning of next six rows. Bind off remaining 10 (18 – 26 -26) sts.

FINISHING

8. Block pieces.

9. With RS facing and dpn, pick up and k 32 (32 – 36 – 40) sts evenly around each leg opening. Join and work in k1, pl rib for three rounds. Bind off in rib. Sew center seam, leaving 1½"/4 cm open at neck.

10. With RS facing and crochet hook, work one row slip st evenly around tail opening.

Option–Step 2

After 14 rows are complete above rib, add opening for harness hook at center of next RS row as follows: work in pattern to center, then yo, k2tog. Continue in pattern to end.

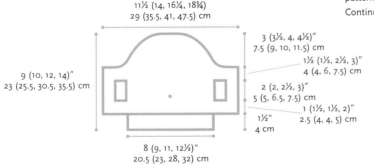

11½ (14, 16¼, 18¾)
29 (35.5, 41, 47.5) cm

3 (3½, 4, 4½)"
7.5 (9, 10, 11.5) cm

1½ (1½, 2½, 3)"
4 (4, 6, 7.5) cm

9 (10, 12, 14)"
23 (25.5, 30.5, 35.5) cm

2 (2, 2½, 3)"
5 (5, 6.5, 7.5) cm

1 (1½, 1½, 2)"
2.5 (4, 4, 5) cm

1½"
4 cm

8 (9, 11, 12½)"
20.5 (23, 28, 32) cm

Puppy Fez

*It's hard to imagine puppies in chapeaux, but apparently it's just
the thing for some stylish pets. This tiny cap is knit from the top
down, and you will learn to do an I-cord technique that you'll use
again and again. Try it, it's like magic!*

●●● **INTERMEDIATE QUICKKNIT**

Circumference (before I-cord border): 20 (24)"/50.5 (61) cm
*Note: After I-cord border, finished circumference is approx 3"/
7.5 cm smaller*

MATERIALS

Worsted weight yarn: 40 yards/35 meters in color A;
20 yards/18 meters each in colors B and C
Double pointed needles (dpns), set of five: size 5 US
(8 UK; 3.75 mm)
Crochet hook: size I US (5 UK; 5.5 mm)

GAUGE

20 sts and 28 rows = 4"/10 cm over St st

✔ *Always check gauge to save time and ensure correct yardage. Adjust
needle size as necessary (see page 4).*

Puppy Profile

NAME: Jenny Lulu, age 1½
BREED: Pug
INTERESTS: Playing with the big
dogs, fetch, and treats of any
and all kinds
STYLE: "Hats are so 'me'. Ears
on the outside, please."
*This beautiful yarn from Brown
Sheep knits like a dream and
holds its shape well—perfect
for Jenny Lulu's chapeau! The
sample photographed is made
from Brown Sheep Naturespun in
#N44 red (A), #861 dark orange
(B), and #245 pink diamond (C).*

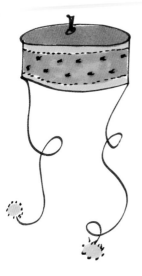

I-CORD TOP

1. With two dpns and A, cast on 4 sts. Work I-cord as follows. *Row 1 (RS)*: k4. *Do not turn work. Slide sts to other end of needle to work next row from RS and k4; rep from * for 2½"/6.5 cm.

CROWN

2. Inc 1 st in each st on next row until there are 8 sts. Divide sts evenly over four dpns (2 sts on each needle). Join and work in rounds of St st (k every rnd), increasing 1 st at end of every needle every rnd (therefore 4 sts increased every rnd) until there are 68 sts, or 17 sts on each needle. See option.

3. For turning ridge, change to C and k one rnd, p four rnds.

4. Continue to k every rnd as follows: four rnds B. *Next rnd*: *k1C, k1A; rep from * around. K four rnds B. *Next rnd*: *k1C, k1A; rep from * around. K four rnds B. Leave sts on needles.

Option–Step 2

To make hat smaller or larger, work a multiple of 4 fewer or 4 more increases.

I-CORD BORDER

5. With two dpns and C, cast on 4 sts and work I-cord as before, attaching cord to lower edge of hat by knitting last st of I-cord together with 1 st from hat. Continue in this way until all sts are bound off.

I-CORD TIES

6. With two dpns and A, cast on 4 sts and work I-cord as before for approx 5½"/14 cm. ***Next row***: k into front and back of next 2 sts and work I-cord on these 4 new sts for approx 3"/7.5 cm. K in front and back of remaining 2 sts and work I-cord on these 4 new sts for approx 3"/7.5 cm.

7. Make a second tie in same way. Attach them to inside of hat under I-cord border. With C, make two 1" (2.5 cm) pom poms and attach to end of ties.

8. Weave in all loose ends. Tie topknot.

Popcorn Pup

*Soft and cozy, this hooded jacket makes an upbeat style state-
ment while keeping the snow at bay. The chest button and under
tummy strap make this petite chic easy to put on and take off.*

●●● **INTERMEDIATE QUICKKNIT**

Finished chest (including straps): 13 (15¼ – 17½)"/
33 (39 – 44.5) cm
Length, neck to tail: 11(12 – 13)"/28 (30.5 – 33) cm

make
larger

MATERIALS

Worsted weight chenille yarn: 130 (165 – 205) yards/117 (148 –
185) meters in main color (MC)
Faux fur: 30 yards/27 meters in contrast color (CC)
Straight needles: sizes 4 and 6 US (10 and 8 UK; 3.5 mm and
4 mm)
Yarn sewing needle
Stitch holder and markers
¾"/2 cm buttons: two

GAUGE

18 sts and 28 rows = 4"/10 cm over St st pattern using
larger needles

*Always check gauge to save time and ensure correct yardage. Adjust
needle size as necessary (see page 4).*

(see page 4)

Puppy Profile

NAME: Einstein, age 1
BREED: Bichon Frise
INTERESTS: Dancing to oldies,
lamb chops, and hanging
around art galleries
STYLE: "I like styles that allow
for free movement. Light and
lively, never constricting."
*Einstein enjoys the ultimate in
comfort, wrapped in Berroco's
Suede, a new and widely
distributed woven chenille,
embellished with Chinchilla faux
fur. The Popcorn embellishments
are done after the knitting is
finished; the bobbles require a
yarn sewing needle and faux fur.*

BODY

1. With larger needles and MC, cast on 32 (38 – 46) sts for lower back edge, then k four rows. Continue in St st as follows. ***Next row (RS)***: k3, inc 1 st in next st, k to last 4 sts, inc 1 st in next st, k3. ***Next row (WS):*** k3, inc 1 st in next st, p to last 4 sts, inc 1 st in next st, k3. Repeat last two rows until there are 44 (50 – 58) sts. Keeping first three and last three sts in garter st and remaining sts in St st, inc 1 st each side (inside three garter sts as before), every eighth (sixth – sixth) row 1 (3 – 4) times, until there are 46 (56 – 66) sts. Work even until piece measures 11 (12 – 13)"/28 (30.5 – 33) cm or desired length. See option.

SHAPE NECK

2. ***Next row (RS):*** keeping first and last 3 sts in garter st and remaining sts in St st, work 12 (16 – 18) sts. Join second ball of yarn and bind off center 22 (24 – 30) sts, then work to end. Working both sides with separate balls, work three rows even. ***Next row (RS):*** k3, k2tog, k to last 5 sts on first half, k2tog, k3; on second half, k3, k2tog, k to last 5 sts, k2tog, k3. ***Next row (WS):*** k3, p to last 3 sts on first half,

Option–Step 1

When piece measures 9 (10 – 11)"/23 (25.5 – 28) cm and before neck shaping, add opening for harness hook at center of next RS row as follows: work in pattern to center, then yo, k2tog. Continue in pattern to end.

k3; work second half in same way. Repeat last two rows 1 (3 – 4) times more—8 sts each side. **Next row (RS)**: k2, k2tog, k2tog, k2 on first half; on second half, k2, k2tog, yo (buttonhole), k2tog, k2. **Next row (WS):** k, dropping yo— 6 sts each side. **Next row (RS)**: k1, k2tog twice, k1. K one row. Bind off remaining 4 sts each side.

HOOD

3. With WS facing, larger needles, and MC, pick up and k36 (38 – 44) sts evenly across neck edge, including 1¼"/3 cm along either side of bound-off sts at neck. **Next row (WS)**: k3, p to last 3 sts, k3. Continue keeping first and last 3 sts in garter st and remaining sts in St st until hood measures 4½"/11.5 cm.

4. With WS facing, place half of sts on a second needle. Fold halves together and k seam as follows. With a third needle, k first st from front needle together with first st from back needle, *k next st from front and back needles together, sl first st over second st to bind off. Repeat from * until all sts are bound off. Cut yarn and pull end through loop.

STRAPS

5. Place markers at side edges of body, approximately 4"/ 10 cm from lower edge of tail (or try on dog to determine placement). With RS facing, smaller needles, and MC, pick up and k8 sts along one side edge above marker. Work in garter st for 2¼"/5.5 cm. **_Next row (buttonhole):_** k2, bind off 4 sts, k to end. K, casting on 4 sts above bound-off sts. K three rows more. Bind off. (If preferred, use Velcro tabs instead of making buttonhole.)

6. Work a second strap in same way along other side, omitting buttonhole.

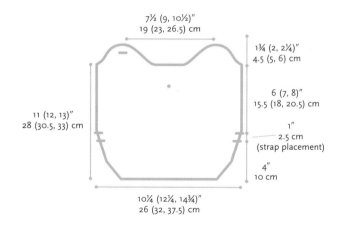

7½ (9, 10½)"
19 (23, 26.5) cm

1¾ (2, 2¼)"
4.5 (5, 6) cm

6 (7, 8)"
15.5 (18, 20.5) cm

1"
2.5 cm
(strap placement)

11 (12, 13)"
28 (30.5, 33) cm

4"
10 cm

10¼ (12¼, 14¾)"
26 (32, 37.5) cm

POPCORNS

7. With faux fur and yarn sewing needle, make popcorns by sewing through fabric six times in same spot, swivelling direction to form round popcorn.

FINISHING

8. Sew one button to strap without buttonhole. Sew one button to neck flap, opposite buttonhole.

Jester

*Rowan is one of the best yarns for a sophisticated color palette,
and this cotton is a fabulous choice for doggies in warmer
climates. This multi-colored treat looks complicated, but you
never work with more than two colors at once.*

●●● **INTERMEDIATE FAIR ISLE**

Finished chest: 12 (13¼ − 15½ − 18)″/30.5 (33.5 − 39.5 − 45.5) cm
Length, neck to tail: 9 (10 − 12 − 14)″/23 (26 − 31 − 35.5) cm

length

MATERIALS

DK weight cotton: 80 (100 − 120 − 150) yards/70 (90 − 110 −
135) meters each of A, B and D; 40 (50 − 60 − 80) yards or
35 (45 − 55 − 70) meters each of C, E, F, G and H
Straight needles: sizes 6 and 7 US (8 and 7 UK; 4 and 4.5 mm)
Circular needle, 16″/40 cm: size 6 US (8 UK; 4 mm)
Double-pointed needles (dpns), set of five: size 6 US
(8 UK; 4 mm)
Stitch holder and markers

GAUGE

20 sts and 25 rows = 4″/10 cm over St st and chart pattern
using larger needles

✓ *Always check gauge to save time and ensure correct yardage. Adjust
needle size as necessary (see page 4).*

(see page 4)

Puppy Profile

NAME: Mocha, age 3
BREED: Long-haired miniature
Dachshund
INTERESTS: Sleeping late,
jousting with cats, bike rides
on sunny days, and lunching on
salmon
STYLE: "I adore mixing colors
and patterns—the brighter, the
better!"
*Mocha's brightly patterned pooch
coverall is made in Rowan's
HankKnit Cotton, a wonderful,
soft, durable cotton available in
exquisite colorways. This sample is
knit in #305 Lavender (A), #287
Blue (B), #219 Light Green (C),
#318 Aqua (D), #314 Purple (E),
#319 Gold (F), #254 Orange (G)
and #215 Red (H).*

BODY

1. With smaller needles and D, cast on 57 (63 – 65 – 71) sts for neck and work in k1, p1 rib for 1.5"/4 cm. Increase 3 (3 – 13 – 19) sts evenly across last (WS) row, to 60 (66 – 78 – 90) sts.

2. Change to larger needles. Work chart pattern in St st until piece measures 2½ (3 – 3 – 3½)" 6.5 (8 – 8 – 9) cm from beginning, ending with a WS row. See option.

SPLIT FOR LEG OPENING

Note: continue to work in chart pattern (repeat rows 1 to 39) to end of piece

3. *Next row (RS)*: work 8 (9 – 10 – 10) sts, then place remaining sts on a holder. Continue on these 8 (9 – 10 – 10) sts only for 2 (2 – 2½ – 2½)"/5 (5 – 6.5 – 6.5) cm, ending with a RS row. Place sts on a second holder. Cut yarn.

Option–Step 2

After 12 rows are complete above rib, add opening for harness hook at center of next RS row as follows: work in pattern to center, then yo, k2tog. Continue in pattern to end.

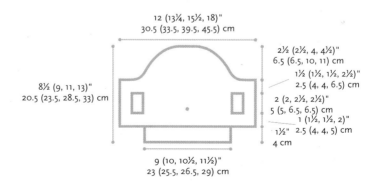

12 (13¾, 15½, 18)"
30.5 (33.5, 39.5, 45.5) cm

2½ (2½, 4, 4½)"
6.5 (6.5, 10, 11) cm

1½ (1½, 1½, 2½)"
2.5 (4, 4, 6.5) cm

2 (2, 2½, 2½)"
5 (5, 6.5, 6.5) cm

1 (1½, 1½, 2)"
1½" 2.5 (4, 4, 5) cm
4 cm

8½ (9, 11, 13)"
20.5 (23.5, 28.5, 33) cm

9 (10, 10½, 11½)"
23 (25.5, 26.5, 29) cm

4. Rejoin yarn and bind off next 7 (7 – 8 – 8) sts from first holder for leg opening, then work next 30 (34 – 42 – 54) sts only for 2 (2 – 2½ – 2½)"/5 (5 – 6.5 – 6.5) cm, ending with a RS row. Place sts on a third holder. Cut yarn.

5. Rejoin yarn and bind off next 7 (7 – 8 – 8) sts from first holder for leg opening. Work remaining 8 (9 – 10 – 10) sts for 2 (2 – 2½ – 2½)"/5 (5 – 6.5 – 6.5) cm, ending with a RS row.

6. ***Next row (WS)***: work 8 (9 – 10 – 10) sts from needle. Cast on 7 (7 – 8 – 8) sts, then work 30 (34 – 42 – 54) sts from third holder. Cast on 7 (7 – 8 – 8) sts, then work remaining 8 (9 – 10 – 10) sts from second holder. Continue on all sts until piece measures 6 (6½ – 7 – 8½)"/15 (17 – 18.5 – 22) cm or desired length from beginning.

Color Key

- Lavender (A)
- Blue (B)
- Lt green (C)
- Aqua (D)
- Purple (E)
- Gold (F)
- Orange (G)
- Red (H)

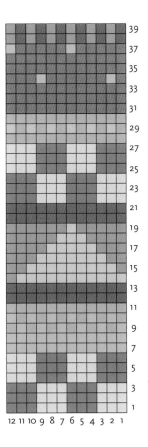

TAIL SHAPING

7. Bind off 4 sts at beginning of next two rows. Decrease 1 st each side every other row 5 (5 – 8 – 8) times. Decrease 1 st each side *every* row 0 (0 – 3 – 6) times. Bind off 3 sts at beginning of next four rows. Bind off remaining 30 (36 – 36 – 42) sts.

FINISHING

8. Block pieces. Sew center seam from neck to beginning of tail shaping.

9. Tail border: with RS facing, circular needle, and D, pick up and k92 (98 – 106 – 114) sts evenly around tail shaping. Work in k1, p1 rib for 1"/2.5 cm. Bind off in rib.

10. Leg borders: with RS facing, dpn, and D, pick up and k34 (34 – 40 – 40) sts evenly around each leg opening. Join and work in k1, p1 rib for 1"/2.5 cm. Bind off in rib.

Collar Cuff

This witty felted collar is a quick and easy project for everyone. The reverse stockinette stripes couldn't be simpler, and the bobbles are worked after the knitting is finished. The felting is fun, too, and the result is adorable. While I always give yardage for simple yarn substitution, I recommend using Brown Sheep or Manos del Uruguay yarn for this project to eliminate surprises in gauge. And you can check the felting time for your own washing machine by felting your gauge swatch first.

● **BEGINNER QUICKKNIT**

Finished circumference (buttoned and after felting): approximately 15"/38 cm

MATERIALS

Worsted weight yarn: 90 yards/80 meters in main color (MC); 5 yards/4.5 meters in contrast color (CC)
Straight needles: size 10.5 US (3 UK; 6.5 mm)
1¼"/3 cm buttons: two

GAUGE

Before felting: 13 sts and 20 rows = 4"/10 cm over St st
After felting: 14 sts and 23 rows = 4"/10 cm

Always check gauge to save time and ensure correct yardage. Adjust needle size as necessary (see page 4).

Puppy Profile

NAME: Lucy, age 4
BREED: Pug
INTERESTS: Motor cross racing, watching tropical fish, visiting McDonald's for French fries
STYLE: "Pink, darling, pink!"

A motor cross groupie, Lucy is snug and stylish in this sumptuous collar, knit in Brown Sheep bulky weight wool. This is a perfect felting yarn and is available in myriad colors. Manos del Uruguay is another perfect felting choice, and the hand-dyed color palette is amazing.

COLLAR

1. With MC, cast on 32 sts. Work in St st for four rows.

2. *Next row (RS)*: *k2tog; rep from * to end. Work on rem 16 sts as follows: *Work five rows in reverse St st. Work five rows in St st; rep from * nine times more, or for desired length.

3. *Next row (RS)*: *Inc 1 st in next st; rep from * to end. Work in reverse St st for four rows. Bind off.

FELTING

4. Due to temperature fluctuations, felting time will vary. Check often for sizing. Set washing machine on hot wash/cold rinse for a small load. Place collar in water with 1 tsp of liquid dishwashing detergent. Run through longest cycle. Check size, then run through again if necessary. Remove, lay flat, and let dry.

FINISHING

5. Cut 1" (2.5 cm) buttonhole on one side of collar. Sew button to corresponding side. Three smaller buttons may be substituted if desired.

DOTS

6. With CC and yarn sewing needle, make dots by sewing six times over the fabric in the same spot, swivelling direction to form round dots. Make dots randomly around collar (see photograph).

Fringe Benefits

*Plaid effects are easily knit in simple stripes, later finished with a
simple crochet counter stripe. Perfect for highland treks or dinner
in the city, this pullover sweater is adorned with fringed trim.*

●●● **INTERMEDIATE QUICKKNIT**

Finished chest (including strap): 13 (15 − 17½)"/33 (38 − 44.5) cm
Length, neck to tail: 11 (12 − 13)"/28 (30.5 − 33) cm

MATERIALS

Worsted weight yarn: 90 (115 − 140) yards/80 (105 − 125)
meters in main color (MC); 30 (35 − 40) yards/25 (32 − 40)
meters in contrast color (CC)
Straight needles: sizes 6 and 8 US (8 and 6 UK; 4 mm and
5 mm)
Crochet hook: size G/6 US (7 UK; 4.5 mm)
Yarn sewing needle
Stitch markers
⅜" (9 mm) buttons: four

GAUGE

16 sts and 22 rows = 4"/10 cm over St st pattern using
larger needles

*Always check gauge to save time and ensure correct yardage. Adjust
needle size as necessary (see page 4).*

Puppy Profile

NAME: Indy, age 1
BREED: Jack Russell Terrier
INTERESTS: Tricks for treats and
pretending to be the RCA dog
STYLE: "Soft and sassy."
*This pooch-in-plaid may look all
innocence, but Indy has a trick or
two up the sleeve of this colorful
concoction knit in Manos del
Uruguay, a hand-spun, hand-dyed
delight with a soft finish. The main
color is #51 teal; the contrast color
is #68 olive.*

BODY

Note: establish then continue to work in stitch pattern while adding increase stitches

1. With larger needles and MC, cast on 28 (33 – 41) sts for lower back edge, then k four rows. **Next row (RS)**: k3, inc 1 st in next st, k5 (3 – 7), [p1, k8] 1 (2 – 2) times, p1, k5 (3 – 7), inc 1 st in next st, k3. **Next row (WS)**: k3, inc 1 st in next st, work pat st to last 4 sts, inc 1 st in next st, k3. Repeat last two rows until there are 40 (45 – 53) sts.

2. Begin stripe and stitch pattern as follows. **Next row (RS)**: with CC, k6 (4 – 8), [p1, k8] 3 (4 – 4) times, p1, k6 (4 – 8). (*Note: the purl stitches should line up.*) **Next row (WS)**: with MC, k3, work in pat st to last 3 sts, k3. Continue in stitch

Stripe Pattern

* One row CC, eleven rows MC; repeat from * for stripe pattern

Stitch Pattern

Row 1 (RS): k8, *p1, k8; repeat from * to end
Row 2 (WS): k3, k all knit sts and p all purl sts to last three stitches, k3
Repeat rows 1 and 2 for stitch pattern

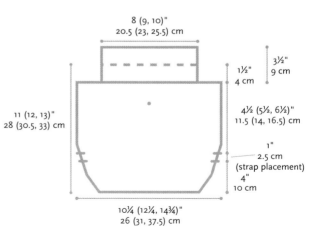

8 (9, 10)"
20.5 (23, 25.5) cm

3½"
9 cm

1½"
4 cm

11 (12, 13)"
28 (30.5, 33) cm

4½ (5½, 6½)"
11.5 (14, 16.5) cm

1"
2.5 cm
(strap placement)
4"
10 cm

10¼ (12¼, 14¾)"
26 (31, 37.5) cm

and stripe pattern as established, and continue to increase 1 st each side (inside of three garter sts as before), every eighth (eighth – sixth) row 1 (2 – 3) times until there are 42 (49 – 59) sts. See option.

3. Work even until piece measures 9½ (10½ – 11½)"/24 (26.5 – 29) cm or desired length. Cut CC. With MC, k next row on RS, dec 3 (4 – 10) sts evenly spaced across until there are 39 (45 – 49) sts. Change to smaller needles and work in k1, p1 rib for 3.5"/9 cm for turtleneck. Bind off loosely in rib.

FINISHING

4. Block piece. With crochet hook and CC, work chain st on top of each vertical line of p sts to form plaid pattern.

STRAPS

5. Place markers at side edges of body approx 4"/10 cm from lower edge of tail (or try on dog to determine placement of straps). With RS facing, smaller needles, and MC, pick up and k8 along one side edge above marker. Work in garter st for 2¼"/5.5 cm. **Next row (buttonhole)**: k2, bind

Option–Step 2

When piece measures 2"/5 cm before the turtleneck, add opening for harness hook at center of next RS row as follows: work in pattern to center, then yo, k2tog. Continue in pattern to end.

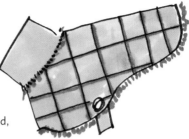

off 4 sts, k to end. K next row, casting on 4 sts over bound-off sts. K two rows more. Bind off. (If preferred, use Velcro tabs instead of making buttonhole.)

6. Work a second strap in same way along other side, omitting buttonhole. Sew button to strap without buttonhole.

7. Sew turtleneck seam. Work short loop with both colors around turtleneck, using a yarn sewing needle and working in and out of the collar edge. Work backstitch between loops to reinforce, if desired. Trim loops to form fringe at desired length. Fold turtleneck in half to RS and sew three buttons around neck (if desired).

Soutache

Dressy and classic, with a touch of European style, these capes are extremely water and snow proof. Knit on larger needles in a looser gauge that is perfect for felting, they work up very quickly. The resulting felted fabric is durable, warm, and washable.

●● **BEGINNER QUICKKNIT**

Add hood.
no trim.

Puppy Profile

NAMES: Bella and Sophia, age 2
BREED: Maltese
INTERESTS: These sisters
both love shopping excursions,
dressing up, light classical
music, and whipped cream.

Finished chest (after felting and including straps): 13½ (16 – 18)"/34.5 (40.5 – 45.5) cm
Length, neck to tail (after felting): 12 (14 – 15)"/30.5 (35.5 – 38) cm

+ length

MATERIALS

Worsted weight yarn: 110 (150 – 180) yards/100 (135 – 162) meters in main color (MC); 10 yards/9 meters in contrast color (CC)
Straight needles: size 10½ US (3 UK, 6.5 mm)
Crochet hook for soutache: size H/7 (6 UK, 5 mm)
Yarn sewing needle
¾" (2 cm) buttons: two

STYLE: "Classic elegance with
touches of whimsy. Our hair
must always be styled just right."
*Not a hair out of place, Bella
and Sophia enjoy showing off
this pretty capelet. It is created in
Manos del Uruguay wool, which
felts like a dream. The soutache
trim is done after felting, giving
the swirls clear definition. The
sample in the photograph is knit
in #03 lavender, with #115 red as
the contrast color.*

GAUGE

Before felting: 13 sts and 20 rows = 4"/10 cm over St st
After felting: 14 sts and 23 rows = 4"/10 cm.

Always check gauge to save time and ensure correct yardage. Adjust needle size as necessary (see page 4).

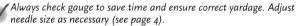

BODY

Note: establish then continue to work in pattern stitch while adding increase stitches

1. With MC, cast on 24 (30 – 36) sts for lower back edge. K four rows. Continue in St st, increasing 1 st (inside k3 edging) each side, every row, six times, until there are 36 (42 – 48) sts. Continue to inc 1 st each side every eighth (eighth – sixth) row 1 (2 – 3) times, until there are 38 (46 – 54) sts. Work even until piece measures 14 (16 – 17)″/35.5 (40.5 – 43) cm or desired length (accounting for shrinking when piece is felted).

NECK SHAPING

2. *Next row (RS):* Work 10 (12 – 14) sts. Join second ball of yarn and bind off center 18 (22 – 26) sts, then work to end. Working both sides with separate balls, work one row even. *Next row (RS)*: k2tog, k to last 2 sts on first half, k2tog; on second half, k2tog, k to last 2 sts, k2tog. Work one row even. Dec 1 st each side every fourth row 2 (2 – 1) times, every second row 0 (1 – 3) times. Bind off remaining 4 sts each side.

STRAPS

3. Place markers at side edges of body approximately 4″/10 cm from lower edge of tail (or try on dog to determine placement). With RS facing and MC, pick up and k6 along one side edge above marker. Work in garter st for 2¾″/7 cm. Bind off.

4. Work a second strap in same way along other side.

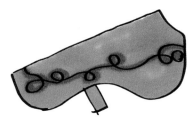

FELTING

5. Due to temperature fluctuations, felting time will vary. Check often for sizing. Set washing machine on hot wash/cold rinse for a small load. Place sweater in water with 1 tsp of liquid dishwashing detergent. Run through longest cycle. Check size, then run through again if necessary. Remove, lay flat, and let dry.

FINISHING

6. With sharp scissors, carefully cut a small buttonhole in one strap and sew button to other strap. Cut another buttonhole 3 sts in from left neck edge. Sew button to other side. See option.

Option–Step 6

If desired, cut a small hole in center of back approximately 2"/5 cm below neck for a harness hook opening.

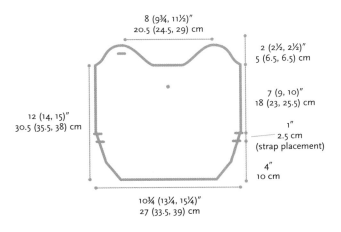

8 (9¾, 11½)"
20.5 (24.5, 29) cm

2 (2½, 2½)"
5 (6.5, 6.5) cm

7 (9, 10)"
18 (23, 25.5) cm

12 (14, 15)"
30.5 (35.5, 38) cm

1"
2.5 cm
(strap placement)

4"
10 cm

10¾ (13¼, 15¼)"
27 (33.5, 39) cm

SOUTACHE

7. With crochet hook and CC, chain approximately 75"/190 cm. Form into swirls and sew onto back of sweater (see photograph).

BOBBLES

8. With CC and yarn sewing needle, make bobbles by sewing through fabric six times in same spot, swivelling direction to form a round bobble. Make bobbles randomly around swirls as desired.

Ruffles Galore

*A ruffle around the edge of this sophisticated cape adds wit,
perfect for your Pomeranian or any other charmer. The ruffles are
worked after the cape is finished, using a long circular needle and
a complementary color.*

●●● **INTERMEDIATE QUICKKNIT**

Finished chest (including straps): 12¾ (14¾ – 16¾)"/32 (37.5 –
42.5) cm
Length, neck to tail: 10 (11 – 12)"/25.5 (28 – 30.5) cm

MATERIALS

Worsted weight yarn: 75 (80 – 100) yards/60 (72 – 90) meters
in main color (MC); 75 (95 – 120) yards/70 (85 – 108) meters
in contrast color (CC)
Straight needles: sizes 6 and 8 US (8 and 6 UK, 4 mm and
5 mm)
20"/50 cm circular needle: size 8 US (6 UK; 5 mm)
Stitch holder and markers
1"/2.5 cm buttons: two

GAUGE

18 sts and 24 rows = 4"/10 cm over St st and chart pattern

*Always check gauge to save time and ensure correct yardage. Adjust
needle size as necessary (see page 4).*

Puppy Profile

NAME: Gussie, age 4
BREED: Pomeranian
INTERESTS: Visits to the local
nursing home. They are so
happy to see me—and they give
me treats!
STYLE: "Colorful and carefree!"
*This perky Pomeranian is all
gussied up in Manos del Uruguay,
a warm, wooly yarn with a
perfect hand. This soft, luxurious
yarn knits like a dream and will
keep your pet dry whatever the
elements. The main color in
the sample is #69 orange; the
contrast color is #M gold.*

BODY

Note: establish then continue to work in pattern stitch while adding increase stitches

1. With larger needles and MC, cast on 31 (37 – 43) sts for lower back edge. Work in St st and chart pattern as follows: work 6-st repeat of chart 5 (6 – 7) times, work last st of chart. Continue as established for one row more.

2. *Next row (RS)*: increase 1 st in first k st, k to last st, then increase 1 st in last st. *Next row (WS):* increase 1 st in first p st, p to last st, then increase 1 st in last p st. Repeat last two rows until there are 43 (49 – 55) sts. Continue and increase 1 st each side every eighth (sixth – sixth) row 1 (3 – 4) times until there are 45 (55 – 63) sts. Work even until

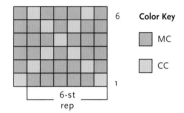

6

Color Key

MC

CC

6-st
rep

1

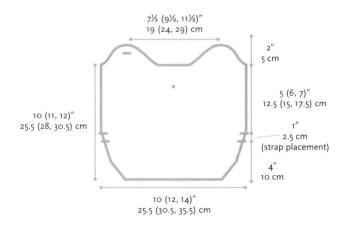

7½ (9½, 11½)"
19 (24, 29) cm

2"
5 cm

5 (6, 7)"
12.5 (15, 17.5) cm

10 (11, 12)"
25.5 (28, 30.5) cm

1"
2.5 cm
(strap placement)

4"
10 cm

10 (12, 14)"
25.5 (30.5, 35.5) cm

piece measures 10 (11 – 12)"/25.5 (28 – 30.5) cm or desired
length.

Option–Step 2

When piece measures 2"/5
cm before neck shaping, add
opening for a harness hook at
center of next RS row as follows:
work in pattern to center, then
yo, k2tog. Continue in pattern
to end.

NECK SHAPING

3. ***Next row (RS):*** work 12 sts. Join second ball of yarn and
bind off center 21 (31 – 39) sts, then work to end. Working
both sides with separate balls, work three rows even. ***Next
row (RS)***: k2tog, k to last 2 sts on first half, k2tog; on second
half, k2tog, k to last 2 sts, k2tog. ***Next row:*** p. Repeat last
two rows once more until there are 8 sts each side.

4. ***Next row (RS)***: k8 on first half; on second half, k2, bind
off 4 sts (buttonhole), k to end. ***Next row:*** p, casting on 4 sts
over bound-off sts on first half, p other half.

5. ***Next row (RS)***: k2, k2tog twice, k2 on first half; work
second half in same way. ***Next row (WS):*** p1, p2tog twice,
p1 on first half; work second half in same way. Bind off
remaining 4 sts each side.

RUFFLE

6. With RS facing, circular needle, and CC, pick up and
k130 (166 – 206) sts evenly around entire outside edge
of sweater. P one row on WS. Inc 1 st in each st (k into
front and back of st) on next row to double the number of
stitches. Continue in k2, p2 for 1"/2.5 cm. Bind off in rib.

STRAPS

7. Place markers at side edges of body approximately 4"/10 cm from lower edge of tail (or try on dog to determine placement). With RS facing, smaller needles, and MC, pick up and k8 along one side edge above marker. Work in garter st for 2¼"/5.5 cm. *Next row (buttonhole)*: k2, bind off 4 sts, k to end. *Next row:* k, casting on 4 sts above bound off sts. K three rows more. Bind off. (If preferred, use Velcro tabs instead of making buttonhole.)

8. Work a second strap in same way along other side, omitting buttonhole.

FINISHING

9. Block piece. Sew one button to strap without buttonhole. Sew one button to neck flap, opposite buttonhole.

Button Up!

Simple stripes make this tiny sweater a true pleasure, and can be knit in a matter of hours. The hand-made fimo buttons from Zecca add instant inimitable color and style.

●● **EASY QUICKKNIT**

Finished chest (including strap): 13¼ (15 – 17½)"/35 (38 – 44.5) cm
Length, neck to tail: 12 (13 – 14)"/30.5 (33 – 36) cm

MATERIALS

Worsted weight yarn: 60 (75 – 95) yards/55 (68 – 85) meters each in main color (MC) and contrast color (CC)
Straight needles: sizes 6 and 8 US (8 and 6 UK; 4 mm and 5 mm)
Stitch holder and markers
Novelty buttons: 11 or 12

GAUGE

16 sts and 22 rows = 4"/10 cm over St st using larger needles

Always check gauge to save time and ensure correct yardage. Adjust needle size as necessary (see page 4).

Puppy Profile

NAME: Linus, age 1
BREED: Toy Poodle
INTERESTS: Pilates, especially the stability ball, running on fresh cut grass, raw organic almonds, ice cubes
STYLE: "Yikes! Stripes!"
Linus looks lively in this neck-to-tail jacket knit in Manos del Uruguay, a gorgeous, soft, and warm yarn. It is available in an amazing array of brightly hued colors, so you can mix and match for your own pooch. In the sample, the main color is #Q medium blue; the contrast color is #04 light blue. The buttons are from www.zecca.net.

BODY

1. With CC, cast on 28 (33 – 41) sts for lower back edge, then k four rows. Work in stripe pattern as follows.

2. ***Next row (RS)***: with MC, k3, inc 1 st in next st, k to last 4 sts, inc 1 st in next st, k3. ***Next row (WS)***: k3, inc 1 st in next st, p to last 4 sts, inc 1 st in next st, k3. Repeat last two rows until there are 40 (45 – 53) sts. Keeping first and last 3 sts in garter st, remaining sts in St st, and all sts in stripe pattern, inc 1 st each side (inside of three garter sts as before), every eighth (eighth – sixth) row 1 (2 – 3) times until there are 42 (49 – 59) sts. Work even until piece measures 10½ (11½ – 12½)"/26.5 (29 – 31.5) cm or desired length, ending with a WS row. See option.

3. ***Next row (RS):*** k. ***Next row (WS):*** k3, p7 (10 – 13), k22 (23 – 27), p7 (10-13), k3. Repeat last two rows once more.

NECK SHAPING

4. Keeping first and last 3 sts in garter st and remaining sts in St st, work 13 (15 – 15) sts. Join second ball of yarn and bind off center 16 (19 – 29) sts, then work to end. Working both sides with separate balls and keeping first and last 3 sts in garter st, work three rows even. ***Next row (RS)***: k3, k2tog, k to last 5 sts on first half, k2tog, k3; on second half, k3, k2tog, k to last 5 sts, k2tog, k3. ***Next row (WS)***: k3, p to last 3 sts on first half, k3; work second half in same way. Repeat last two rows 1 (2 – 2) times more until there are 9 sts each side.

5. ***Next row (RS)***: k3, k3tog , k3 on first half; work second half in same way. ***Next row (WS):*** k3, p1, k3. ***Next row (RS)***: k2, k3tog, k2 on first half; on second half, k2, yo (buttonhole), k3tog, k2. K next row, dropping yo—5 sts each side.

Option—Step 2

When piece measures 2"/5 cm before neck shaping, add opening for a harness hook at center of next RS row as follows: work in pattern to center, then yo, k2tog. Continue in pattern to end.

Stripe Pattern

* Eight rows MC, 6 rows CC; repeat from * for stripe pattern

6. *Next row (RS)*: k2tog, k1, k2tog on each side. *Next row (WS)*: k3tog and fasten off last st each side.

STRAPS

7. Place markers at side edges of body approximately 4"/10 cm from lower edge of tail (or try on dog to determine placement). With RS facing, smaller needles, and CC, pick up and k8 along one side edge above marker. Work in garter st for 2¼"/5.5 cm. *Next row (buttonhole)*: k3, yo, k2tog, k to end, K three rows more. Bind off.

8. Work a second strap in same way along other side, omitting buttonhole.

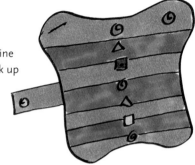

FINISHING

9. Block piece. Sew one button to strap without buttonhole. Sew one button to neck flap, opposite buttonhole. Sew remaining buttons down center of back (see photograph).

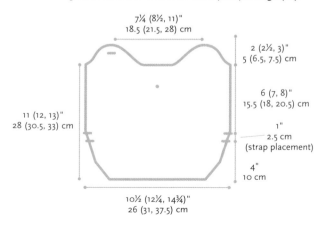

7¼ (8½, 11)"
18.5 (21.5, 28) cm

2 (2½, 3)"
5 (6.5, 7.5) cm

6 (7, 8)"
15.5 (18, 20.5) cm

11 (12, 13)"
28 (30.5, 33) cm

1"
2.5 cm
(strap placement)

4"
10 cm

10½ (12¼, 14¾)"
26 (31, 37.5) cm

Puppy Panache

This toasty sweater jacket has loads of uptown style. The yarn is line-dyed in stripes of different colors, so there is no need to change yarns. The chenille faux fur collars adds a touch of sophistication.

●● **EASY QUICKKNIT**

Finished chest (including strap): 13 (15¼ – 17½)"/33 (39 – 44.5) cm
Length, neck to tail: 11 (12 – 13)"/28 (30.5 – 33) cm

MATERIALS

Worsted weight yarn: 95 (115 – 145) yards/85 (105 – 130) meters in main color (MC)
Faux fur: 35 (45 – 60) yards/30 (40 – 55) meters in contrast color (CC)
Straight needles: sizes 6 and 8 US (8 and 6 UK; 4 mm and 5 mm)
Stitch holder and markers
¾"/2 cm buttons: two

GAUGE

18 sts and 26 rows = 4"/10 cm over St st and worsted weight yarn, using larger needles
12 sts = 4¼"/11 cm and 16 rows = 4"/10 cm over St st and two strands of faux fur, using larger needles

Always check gauge to save time and ensure correct yardage. Adjust needle size as necessary (see page 4).

Puppy Profile

NAME: Roxie, age 3
BREED: Jack Russell Terrier
INTERESTS: Prime rib, pizza, sunbathing, and squirrel sports
STYLE: "I'm all about color. No plain-Jane pales or pastels for me."

Berroco's color-spaced wool and acrylic mix, trimmed with furry Chinchilla, makes for rather a chic take on doggie attire. The yarn changes color as the ball unrolls, creating an automatic rainbow of color. The main color—which creates stripes from red to green to yellow to purple, as in the photograph—is Berroco Foliage #5961; the contrast color is Berroco Chinchilla #5520.

BODY

1. With larger needles and MC (sample is line-dyed multicolor yarn), cast on 32 (38 – 46) sts for lower back edge, then k four rows. Continue in St st as follows.

2. **Next row (RS)**: k3, inc 1 st in next st, k to last 4 sts, inc 1 st in next st, k3. **Next row (WS)**: k3, inc 1 st in next st, p to last 4 sts, inc 1 st in next st, k3. Repeat last two rows until there are 44 (50 – 58) sts. Keeping first and last 3 sts in garter st and remaining sts in St st, inc 1 st each side (inside of 3 garter sts as before), every eighth (sixth – sixth) row 1 (3 – 4) times until there are 46 (56 – 66) sts. Work even until piece measures 11 (12 – 13)″/28 (30.5 – 33) cm or desired length, ending with a WS row. See option.

Option—Step 2

When piece measures 2″/5 cm before neck shaping, add opening for a harness hook at center of next RS row as follows: work in pattern to center, then yo, k2tog. Continue in pattern to end.

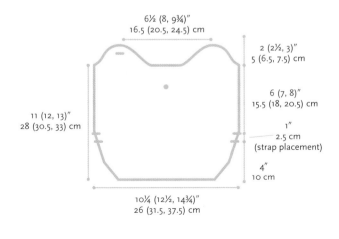

6½ (8, 9¾)″
16.5 (20.5, 24.5) cm

2 (2½, 3)″
5 (6.5, 7.5) cm

6 (7, 8)″
15.5 (18, 20.5) cm

11 (12, 13)″
28 (30.5, 33) cm

1″
2.5 cm
(strap placement)

4″
10 cm

10¼ (12½, 14¾)″
26 (31.5, 37.5) cm

NECK SHAPING

3. Keeping first and last 3 sts in garter st and remaining sts in St st, work 16 (20 – 22) sts. Join second ball of yarn and bind off center 14 (16 – 22) sts, then work to end. Working both sides with separate balls, work one row even. **Next row (RS)**: k3, k2tog, k to last 5 sts on first half, k2tog, k3; on second half, k3, k2tog, k to last 5 sts, k2tog, k3. **Next row (WS):** k3, p to last 3 sts on first half, k3; work second half in same way. Repeat last two rows 3 (5 – 6) times more until there are 8 sts each side.

4. **Next row (RS)**: k2, k2tog twice, k2 on first half; on second half, k2, k2tog, yo (buttonhole), k2tog, k2. K next row, dropping yo—6 sts each side. (If preferred, use Velcro tabs instead of making buttonholes.)

5. **Next row (RS)**: k1, k2tog twice, k1. K one row. Bind off remaining 4 sts each side.

COLLAR

6. With CC, pick up and k39 (45 – 55) sts evenly around neck edge. Work in St st for 2½"/6.5cm. On RS, bind off very loosely.

STRAPS

7. Place markers at side edges of body approximately 4"/10 cm from lower edge of tail (or try on dog to determine placement). With RS facing, smaller needles, and MC, pick up and k8 along one side edge above marker. Work in garter st for 2¼"/5.5 cm. **Next row (buttonhole):** k2, bind off 4 sts, k to end. K next row, casting on 4 sts over bound-off sts. K two rows more. Bind off.

8. Work a second strap in same way along other side, omitting buttonhole.

FINISHING

9. Block piece. Sew one button to strap without buttonhole. Sew one button to neck flap, opposite buttonhole.

69

Pom Pom

*This color-blocked charmer is easily worked by adding another
ball of yarn of the main color for the intarsia. The simple cables
add interest and dimension as well.*

●●● **INTERMEDIATE QUICKKNIT**

Finished chest: 12 (14 – 16 – 18)"/30.5 (35.5 – 40.5 – 45.5) cm
Length, neck to tail: 10 (12 – 13 – 15)"/25.5 (31 – 33.5 – 37.5) cm

MATERIALS

Worsted weight yarn: 55 (75 – 95 – 120) yards/50 (65 – 85 –
110) meters in color A; 50 (70 – 85 – 110) yards/45 (63 – 75 –
100) meters in color B; 20 yards/10 meters in color C
Straight needles: sizes 6 and 8 US (8 and 6 UK; 4 mm and
5 mm)
Double pointed needles (dpns), set of five: sizes 6 and 8 US
(8 and 6 UK; 4 mm and 5 mm)
Cable needle (cn)
Crochet hook: size H/8 (6 UK; 5 mm)
Stitch holder and markers

GAUGE

18 sts and 24 rows = 4"/10 cm over St st using larger needles
26 sts = 3½"/9 cm over cable panel using larger needles

✓ *Always check gauge to save time and ensure correct yardage. Adjust
needle size as necessary (see page 4).*

Puppy Profile

NAME: Boscoe, age 4
BREED: Miniature Short-haired
Dachshund
INTERESTS: Classic cars, fifties
music, frozen yogurt
STYLE: "Retro hip, definitely."
*Boscoe is playfully chic in this
spirited yet casual concoction. It's
a favorite for outings to his father's
antique car dealership, Goldenrod
Garage. Pom Pom is knit in Brown
Sheep Lamb's Pride Worsted,
#M190 teal for color A, # M120
lime green for color B and #M81
hot pink for color C*

71

Cable Panel

(OVER 26 STITCHES)

Row 1 (RS): p2, *k6, p2; repeat from *

Rows 2, 4, 6, AND 8: k all knit sts and p all purl sts

Row 3: p2, *sl 3 sts to cn and hold to back of work, k3, k3 from cn, p2; repeat from *

Rows 5 AND 7: repeat row 1

Repeat rows 1 to 8 for cable panel

BODY

1. With smaller needles and color A, cast on 55 (59 – 63 – 69) sts for neck and work in k1, p1 rib for 1½ (1½ – 2 – 2)"/ 4 (4 – 5 – 5) cm, increasing 9 (15 – 19 – 23) sts evenly across last (WS) row until there are 64 (74 – 82 – 92) sts.

2. Change to larger needles. Cut A and work in pattern as follows. Join B, work 19 (24 – 28 – 33) sts in St st. Join A and work next 26 sts in cable panel. Join second ball of B and work remaining 19 (24 – 28 – 33) sts in St st. Continue in colors and patterns as established until piece measures 2½ (3 – 3½ – 4)"/6.5 (7.5 – 9 – 10) cm, ending with a WS row. See option.

SPLIT FOR LEG OPENING

3. *Next row (RS)*: work 7 (8 – 9 – 9) sts, then place remaining stitches on a holder. Continue on these 7 (8 – 9 – 9) sts only for 2 (2½ – 2½ – 3)"/5 (6.5 – 6.5 – 7.5) cm, ending with a RS row. Place stitches on a second holder. Cut yarn.

4. Rejoin yarn and bind off next 6 (6 – 7 – 7) sts from first holder for leg opening, then work next 38 (46 – 50 – 60) sts only for 2 (2½ – 2½ – 3)"/5 (6.5 – 6.5 – 7.5) cm, ending with a RS row. Place stitches on a third holder. Cut yarn.

5. Rejoin yarn and bind off next 6 (6 – 7 – 7) sts from first holder for leg opening, then work remaining 7 (8 – 9 – 9) sts only for 2 (2½ – 2½ – 3)"/5 (6.5 – 6.5 – 7.5) cm, ending with a RS row.

6. *Next row (WS)*: work 7 (8 – 8 – 9) sts from needle, cast on 6 (6 – 7 – 7) sts, work 38 (46 – 52 – 60) sts from third

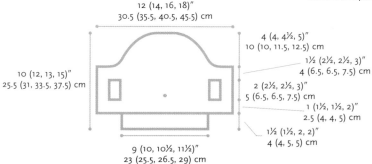

holder, cast on 6 (6 – 7 – 7) sts, work rem 7 (8 – 9 – 9) sts from second holder. Continue on all stitches until piece measures 6 (8 – 8½ – 10)″/15.5 (20.5 – 21.5 – 25.5) cm or desired length.

TAIL SHAPING

7. Bind off 6 (8 – 9 – 10) sts at beginning of next two rows. Decrease 1 st each side every other row 5 (5 – 6 – 7) times and every row 6 (6 – 8 – 8) times. Bind off 4 sts at beginning of next six rows. Bind off remaining 6 (12 – 12 – 18) sts.

FINISHING

8. Block pieces.

9. Leg bands: with RS facing, dpn, and color A, pick up and k30 (34 – 36 – 40) sts evenly around each leg opening. Join and work in k1, p1 rib for three rounds. Bind off in rib. Sew center seam, leaving 1.5″/4 cm open at neck.

Option–Step 2

After 12 rows are complete above rib, add opening or a harness hook at center of next RS row as follows: work in pattern to center, then yo, k2tog. Continue in pattern to end.

12 (14, 16, 18)″
30.5 (35.5, 40.5, 45.5) cm

4 (4, 4½, 5)″
10 (10, 11.5, 12.5) cm

1½ (2½, 2½, 3)″
4 (6.5, 6.5, 7.5) cm

2 (2½, 2½, 3)″
5 (6.5, 6.5, 7.5) cm

1 (1½, 1½, 2)″
2.5 (4, 4, 5) cm

10 (12, 13, 15)″
25.5 (31, 33.5, 37.5) cm

1½ (1½, 2, 2)″
4 (4, 5, 5) cm

9 (10, 10½, 11½)″
23 (25.5, 26.5, 29) cm

Boss Tweed

The perfect beginner pattern, this pullover fits many shapes and body sizes. It's worked in one simple piece, and sews together for a perfect fit, given the simple stockinette pattern.

●● **ADVANCED BEGINNER QUICKKNIT**

Finished chest: 12 (13½ – 15½ – 18)"/30.5 (34.5 – 39.5 – 45.5) cm
Length, neck to tail: 9½ (10½ – 12½ – 13½)"/24 (26.5 – 31.5 – 34) cm

MATERIALS

Worsted weight yarn: 65 (80 – 100 – 130) yards/60 (70 – 90 – 120) meters
Straight needles: sizes 8 and 9 US (6 and 5 UK; 5 mm and 5.5 mm)
Double-pointed needles (dpns), set of five: size 6 US (8 UK; 4 mm)
16"/40 cm circular needle: size 6 US (8 UK; 4 mm)
Stitch holder and markers

GAUGE

15 sts and 22 rows = 4"/10 cm over St st using larger needles

Always check gauge to save time and ensure correct yardage. Adjust needle size as necessary (see page 4).

Add length and diameter

Puppy Profile

NAME: Emmet Apple, age 2
BREED: Chihuahua
INTERESTS: Jazz music, rough housing with my older brothers, and ballet lessons
STYLE: "Cautiously conservative."

Emmet Apple is wrapped from collar to tail in this baby alpaca blend from the Fiber Exchange. This is a brand new and fabulous yarn spun in Maine from North American alpaca wool.

BODY

1. With smaller needles, cast on 41 (43 – 45 – 49) sts for neck and work in k1, p1 rib for 2½ (2½ – 3 – 3)"/6.5 (6.5 – 7.5 – 7.5) cm, increasing 5 (7 – 13 – 19) sts evenly across last (WS) row until there are 46 (50 – 58 – 68) sts.

2. Change to larger needles. Work in St st until piece measures 3½ (4 – 4½ – 5)"/9 (10 – 11.5 – 12.5) cm, ending with a WS row. See option.

SPLIT FOR LEG OPENING

3. ***Next row (RS)***: work 7 (8 – 9 – 10) sts, then place remaining sts on a holder. Continue on these 7 (8 – 9 – 10) sts only for 2 (2 – 2 – 2½)"/5 (5 – 5 – 6.5) cm, ending with a RS row. Place stitches on a second holder. Cut yarn.

4. Rejoin yarn and bind off next 5 (6 – 6 – 7) sts from first holder for leg opening, then work next 22 (22 – 28 – 34) sts only for 2 (2 – 2 – 2½)"/5 (5 – 5 – 6.5) cm, ending with a RS row. Place sts on a third holder. Cut yarn.

Option–Step 2

After 12 rows have been worked above rib, add opening for a harness hook at center of next RS row as follows: work in pattern to center, then yo, k2tog. Continue in pattern to end.

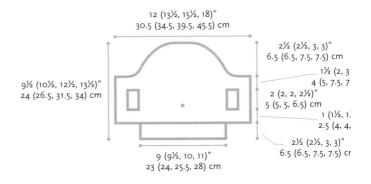

12 (13½, 15½, 18)"
30.5 (34.5, 39.5, 45.5) cm

2½ (2½, 3, 3)"
6.5 (6.5, 7.5, 7.5) cm

1½ (2, 3
4 (5, 7.5, 7

2 (2, 2, 2½)"
5 (5, 5, 6.5) cm

1 (1½, 1.
2.5 (4, 4,

2½ (2½, 3, 3)"
6.5 (6.5, 7.5, 7.5) cr

9½ (10½, 12½, 13½)"
24 (26.5, 31.5, 34) cm

9 (9½, 10, 11)"
23 (24, 25.5, 28) cm

5. Rejoin yarn and bind off next 5 (6 – 6 – 7) sts from first holder for leg opening, then work remaining 7 (8 – 9 – 10) sts only for 2 (2 – 2 – 2½")/5 (5 – 5 – 6.5) cm, ending with a RS row.

6. *Next row (WS)*: work 7 (8 – 9 – 10) sts from needle, cast on 5 (6 – 6 – 7) sts, work 22 (22 – 28 – 34) sts from third holder, cast on 5 (6 – 6 – 7) sts, work rem 7 (8 – 9 – 10) sts from second holder. Continue on all sts until piece measures 7 (8 – 9½ – 10½")/18 (20.5 – 24 – 26.5) cm, or desired length.

TAIL SHAPING

7. Bind off 7 (8 – 9 – 10) sts at beginning of next two rows. Dec 1 st each side every other row 6 (6 – 7 – 7) times. Bind off remaining 20 (22 – 26 – 34) sts.

FINISHING

8. Block pieces. Sew center seam from neck to beginning of tail shaping.
9. Tail border: With RS facing and circular needle, pick up and k54 (60 – 66 – 76) sts evenly around tail shaping. Work in k1, p1 rib for 1/2"/1.5 cm. Bind off in rib.
10. Leg bands: with RS facing and dpn, pick up and k20 (22 – 22 – 26) sts evenly around each leg opening. Join and work in k1, p1 rib for three rounds. Bind off in rib.

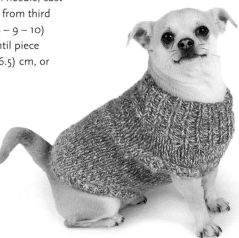

Team & Thanks

First there was the idea, then the fast and furious knitting, then the clamorous photo shoots filled with barking, dancing dogs, then the writing, editing, and technical wizardry . . . and I am always so grateful to my cheery bunch of extremely talented co-workers. *Nina Fuller* takes all the extraordinary photos. *Carla Scott* is the brilliant technical editor who writes and edits the patterns. *Isabel Smiles* is my design lieutenant. *Tunde Schwartz* is my extraordinary studio assistant, keeping everything organized and moving forward as well as adding her creative input. Thanks everyone— you're the best!

JIL EATON

Jil's first dog was Jeff, an enormous white English Bulldog, followed by Boy, a Labrador stray. Then came Samantha, the 125-pound German Shepherd. Another stray, Nina, was a beautiful Husky with China-blue eyes. Then Sam, a lop-eared Shepherd appeared on the scene, and Jil married his owner, David. Finally, along came Zachary, the giant, soulful Great Dane/Pointer/Greyhound mix, who still shares Jil's life.

Educated in art at Skidmore College, Colby College and the Graduate School of Design at Harvard University, Jil's career as painter and graphic designer finally succumbed to her early fashion instincts. She designs, publishes, and distributes internationally an independent line of hand-knitting patterns under the Minnowknits™ label. A formidable knitter, Jil Eaton's designs have a comfortable, chic silhouette, melding the traditional with the new, adapting everything in easy-to-knit projects with great attention to detail, fresh styling, and unusual colorways. Jil produces two pattern collections annually, designs for *Vogue Knitting International* and other publications, and is busy with her eighth book.

NINA FULLER

Nina Fuller, whose sense of style and fashion is inimitable, is the one who so wonderfully captures all these charming doggie models on film. A nationally acclaimed location and studio photographer, Nina has degrees from Silvermine College of Art and George Washington University in Photography, Painting, and Printmaking. Always with a camera in hand, Nina has a gift for catching the right angle, finding the most beautiful light. Nina's clients include LL Bean, Land's End, Horse & Hound, the Boston Globe, and Atlantic Records. She lives in Maine with her two children, two horses, and furry Murphy, a Peke-a-Poo.

ISABEL SMILES

Isabel Smiles, design guru as well as location stylist, moved to Maine years ago after a successful run as a stylist and antiques & design shop owner in New York and Connecticut. She created the world-renowned Pomegranate Inn Bed and Breakfast, a stunning small hotel in Portland, Maine. She continues to do select freelance styling for the Meredith Corporation and Hearst Publications, as well as private design commissions. She is currently sans pooch, but spent many years with Nutmeg, a mop-head with enormous charm.

CARLA SCOTT

Carla Scott is my pattern writer, technical editor and general knitting wizard. Carla is without peer in her fabulous knowledge of knitting and garment structure, and since the beginning has been able to translate my design concepts into written instructions and comprehensive charts. She is energized with each new design challenge, figuring out engineering details with aplomb. She is clear and calm amidst a mountain of math and engineering, and has a design eye as well. Carla is Executive Editor at *Vogue Knitting*, and clearly understands fashion as well as knitting; working with her is always delightful. She lives in New York City with her husband, daughter, and pet fish.

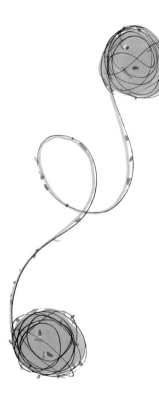

TUNDE SCHWARTZ

Tunde Schwartz, my studio assistant, is worth her weight in gold. Fresh from the Big Apple after years as a model, her fashion sense is hip, fresh, and gorgeous. Not only an extraordinary organizer and studio manager, she is also a stylist, wordsmith, fashionista, and Pilates teacher. Invaluable. She lives in Maine with her husband and two darling daughters.

THE KNITTERS

I am blessed to have hand knitters with such professional craftsmanship. Knitting prototypes is tricky, and this pup collection was quite a challenge, given odd shapes and sizing. Knitting under deadline can be an ordeal, but these garments have been perfectly done. Big thanks to *Nita Young*, *Lucinda Heller*, *Shirley LaBranch*, *Pam Tessier*, and *Carol Lawrence*.

THE MODELS

It ups the ante when animals are included in a photo shoot, and this project was no exception. Small in stature but big in personality, these doggie models charmed us all!

Cabled Delight: Griffin, a Yorkie
Puppy Fez: Jennie LuLu, a fawn Pug
Popcorn Pup: Einstein, a Bichon Frise
Jester: Mocha, a long-haired miniature Dachshund
Fringe Benefits: Indy, a Jack Russell Terrier
Soutache: Bella and Sophia, Maltese sisters
Collar Cuff: Lucy, a black Pug
Ruffles Galore: Gussie, a Pomeranian
Button-Up! Linus, a Toy Poodle
Puppy Panache: Roxie, a Jack Terrier
Pom Pom: Boscoe, a short-haired Dachshund
Boss Tweed: Emmet Apple, a Chihuahua

Thanks to *Bow Wow Sophistique*, a delightful pet shop in Portland, Maine, for the loan of adorable canine props. Visit www.bowwowsophistique.com.

Last but absolutely not least, enormous thanks go to my ever brilliant and esteemed publisher, Anne Knudsen of Breckling Press, and to my enormously talented art director, Kim Bartko of Bartko Design. Thanks also to my mother, Nancy Whipple Lord, for teaching me to knit, and to my grandmother Flora Hall Whipple for teaching her to knit.

Stockists

All the gorgeous yarns and products used in this book are available from the following distributors. You can depend on any of these labels for yarns that are of the highest quality, some of the most beautiful yarns on the market. Contact them for shops in your area, or check their websites.

YARNS

Berroco
14 Elmdale Road
PO Box 367
Uxbridge, MA 01569-0367
508-278-2527
www.berroco.com

Manos Del Uruguay
Design Source,
US Distributor
38 Montvale, Suite 145
Stoneham, MA 02180
888-566-9970

Rowan Yarns from Westminster Fibers
5 Northern Boulevard
Amherst, NH 03031
603-886-5041
www.knitrowan.com

NEEDLES

Addi Turbos from Skacel Collection, Inc.
224 SW 12th Street
Renton, WA 98055
213-854-2710

BUTTONS

Zecca
(Hand-made Fimo buttons)
PO Box 1664
Lakeville, CT 06039
860-435-2211
www.zecca.net

Central Yarn
53 Oak Street
Portland, ME 04101
207-775-0852
www.centralyarn.com

Knitters' Abbreviations

approx	Approximately
beg	Beginning
CC	Contrasting color
cont	Continue(ing)s
CN	Cable needle
Dec(s)	Decrease(s)
dpn	Double-pointed needle
est	Established
garter	Knit all stitches and/or rows
inc(s)	Increase(s)
k	Knit
k2tog	Knit two stitches together
M1	Make one stitch
MC	Main color
p	Purl
p2tog	Purl two stitches together
pat(s)	Patterns(s)
psso	Pass the slipped stitch over the last stitch worked

rem	Remaining
rep	Repeat(s)
rev St st	Reverse stockinette stitch--k all WS rows, p all RS rows
rib	Rib(bing)
rnd(s)	Round(s) in circular knitting
RS	Right side
SKP	slip 1, knit 1, pass slipped stitch over
sl	Slip(ed) (ping). Slip stitches from left hand needle to right hand needle
ssk	Slip 1, slip 1, knit 1
st(s)	Stitch(es)
St st	Stockinette stitch--k all RS rows, p all WS rows
tog	Together
WS	Wrong side

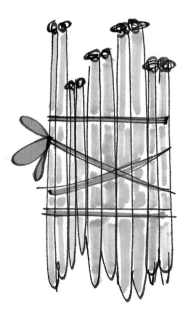

Needle Conversions

METRIC (MM)	US	OLD UK
2	0	14
2.25	1	13
2.5		
2.75	2	12
3		
3.25	3	10
3.5	4	
3.75		
4	6	8
4.5	7	7
5	8	6
5.5	9	5
6	10	4
6.5	10.5	3
7		2
7.5		1
8	11	0
9	13	00
10	15	000